The Next Critical Step

The Next Critical Step

Bernard Theroux

Morning Light Publications

The Next Critical Step
Copyright © 1995 by Bernard Theroux
All rights reserved

ISBN 0-9645910-0-6

Morning Light Publications
P.O. Box 15341
Seattle, Washington 98115-0341

Acknowledgements

I am deeply grateful to the following people for their love and support during the period in which this book was developed and completed: To Norman and Jeanette Carlson for literally opening their home to me and to Jeanette for being the first to review the manuscript. To my mother for her steady presence, to Karen S. Isaksen for her insightful feedback and review, to Dan Gedosch and Sikata Banerjee, Maurine Weaver, and Darryl Klippsten for their invaluable support and friendship, to Rick and Judi Cook for their assistance with proofreading, and to James Morse for his generous help with typesetting.

Introduction

When you ignore that voice within, the longing of your soul, regarding what you are to do with your life, then frustration develops. If you use spiritual practices to help you to quiet those frustrations, what do you think will eventually occur? Perhaps the frustration, the creative urging from within, this powerful sense that your life will and must change, emerges from a deep knowing within.

These pages explore the possibility that acting upon your purpose may be the next critical step in the spiritual process for you and many other people. It is not suggested that meditation and prayer be replaced with the active life, but it is being suggested that there comes a point in which the meditative life will deepen no further until the individual begins to actually act in the world in a very specific manner. The form of this action depends entirely upon the purpose towards which the individual is being directed. Only this action, which is unique to the individual and a sign of true faith, will provide a sense of meaning. This action, multiplied in the lives of countless numbers of people throughout the world, is the action which can make a difference. This is the global manifestation of spirit into the Earth plane, and you have a special part in it.

Imagine a traveler. He is not a vacationer. He has a purpose for his travels. He is traveling in undeveloped parts of the world, and often traverses wide expanses which have little in the way of modern modes of transportation. Sometimes he must walk, ride in animal drawn carts, bounce in old buses and never can he rely upon arriving at his destination at a predictable time.

Our traveler is collecting information, and each new step along his journey sheds light on what he is moved to attempt next. His overall purpose seems quite clear; yet, he is always needing to adjust and be flexible. He has been traveling for an extended period of time and is tired. He comes to a small village which he finds especially pleasant, and he settles down there for a time to rest his weary bones and contemplate his life. He is so exhausted from his travels that he begins to doubt his purpose. Perhaps he should simply remain in this comfortable village for an extended time and settle into a more ordinary existence. It is so tiring out on the open road; wouldn't it be better to just stay in one place for once.

Our traveler is at a way station in the path of his life. Clearly moved by a sense of purpose, he nonetheless has grown tired and doubtful. Yet, as attractive as this way station appears to him, he eventually begins to hear that voice within him calling out once again. That voice is drawing him back, not letting him rest. He cannot fulfill his purpose from this safe way station. How long will he remain at this safe haven? Who knows?

Everyone is on a journey, and everyone hears the calling of that voice inside which is prompting them, now and again, to travel on and return to the open road. The nature of that calling and the willingness to listen to that voice varies from person to person. Many find comfort in simply letting their life remain as it is. Daily life becomes their way station, and they choose for the period of this lifetime, to never return to the road. The voice within never dies, but it is pushed aside until it is rarely heard again. It must find more covert ways to communicate so that one day, in the future, the individual will begin to listen once more.

Way stations are perhaps a necessity in the journey of our life, but when we make a way station into a way of life, we have then lost touch with our soul's impulse to use this life experience to advance itself and to contribute to the common good. One man's way station is another man's route of adventure. Only you know for sure if you are resting too long in one place. Only you can really know if you are listening to the voice of your soul and doing as best as you can to listen to this most intimate guidance. It is not revealing to compare people. We must know what one's inner longing truly is, and then we can look to see how the outer life is being lived. The mere outer form of our life conveys only a partial picture. When we understand something of a person's deep longings which spring from the depths of their soul, then we can look at their outer actions and have a context to place them in.

What might look from the outside to be a very creative life, may in fact be a stagnant existence for the person living it. On the other hand, a person's life may look relatively unimpressive to the eyes of your ego, and yet, in fact, it could be a life full of real growth and development.

The inner and the outer are not truly separate. The human experience is not to be avoided, and your deep inner voice will guide you to those aspects of the human journey that are best suited to your spiritual development. When we say that the human experience is not to be avoided, that does not mean that all the choices within the range of human experience will serve your development. Once again, you have to take your individual life into account. There is nothing inherently worthy about indulging in life experiences that you have already outgrown. These habit patterns are nothing more than the way stations along the road. Many choose to remain at these way stations, and there is no condemnation of this choice. However, the way of growth is the way of the open road.

For a significant number of people the life style of modern, middle class life, has become something that they have outgrown. These people are looking for a way to return to the open road once again. They are not truly enamored any longer with traditional marriage, jobs, settling down in a comfortable house for the rest of their life, and so on. Their consciousness has already risen above the marketplace consciousness that drives the machine of modern culture, and these people often feel as though they are strangers in a foreign land. More than that, they also feel at times as though they are strangers even to themselves. "What is this strange side of me that seems to be taking over my life?", they may wonder. "Why can't I be satisfied anymore with life as I have lived it to now? What is wrong with me?" In other moments, more sure of themselves, they might state, "I must change things in my life. I have to listen to my heart even if it means that I may disappoint those in my life who would like to see me stay just as I am. I have to listen to my heart even if I think that I am crazy sometimes." If you can relate to these thoughts, you may be longing to return to the open road. Perhaps you were on the open road, and now simply find that you have been in a way station longer than needed. You are itching to grow again, and yet, it can be frightening.

Way stations can begin to look like the only life possible. To leave can even look and feel like dying. Clearly, only a deep longing for freedom can call us out. Our soul thrives on true freedom, and if we were to be honest with ourselves, we would have to admit that freedom is one of our deepest desires. True freedom is the antithesis of selfishness. The ego may try to talk you out of continuing your life journey by making you feel that it would be selfish to listen to your heart. We end up feeling guilty about who we really are, and we feel guilty about what we want to do. This reversal often occurs: We mistake the voice of fear for the voice of truth, and we say that the voice of truth is a devil of sorts, tempting us away from the reasonable life. For this reason, we may have to experience the utter collapse of our way station. Sometimes we require crisis to wake us up. However, crisis alone will not send us on our way. After the crisis passes, we will simply return to the way we used to live unless we have arrived at the point where we are no longer so attracted to what our particular way station has to offer.

I magine that you are entering a spacious and sacred room. The artwork, carpet, lighting, plants and the atmosphere itself draws you into a state of of great peace and quietude. Within this special place are people of great wisdom. These men and women are placed throughout the room, and they appear to be calmly absorbed in the moment. They clearly are not preparing to go anywhere. It occurs to you, with certainty, that these wise men and wise women are there for you. You notice a wooden ladder at a far corner of this large room. Even the ladder was made with great care; it is an art piece all of its own. Knowing what to do, you approach the ladder and climb it. You find yourself in a loft from which you can look down and view the wise men and women below. Though you are close and in the same room with them, you somehow feel as though you are far away, on a mountain top, able to observe those below, but they cannot see you. There are two comfortable chairs in the loft, placed close to one another.

With infinite patience, the people of wisdom will wait until you have had an opportunity to be visited by each one of them. One by one, they will enter the loft and take a seat next to you. Time will stop as you ask questions of, listen to, and sit quietly with each wise woman and wise man. Some move you most by what they say to you, some by what they ask of you, some by how they gaze at you, and some by the depth and peace of their silence. Nothing is rushed. Time is meaningless while this visitation occurs. After each visit a perfect amount of time is allowed before the next wise person climbs the ladder to meet with you.

During one of these intervals some important insights begin to make themselves known to you. Clearly you are in the midst of a great spiritual blessing, but how do you know that this is so? Isn't it possible that there are many people who would have entered this room, walked around and then left, perhaps finding the gathering of men and women to be a bit odd, and who would not have seen the sacred nature of the gathering? What is it within yourself, you wonder, that even recognizes the value of this event? How do you recognize something unless you already have a familiarity with it? If you went to look for your car in a large parking lot, you would never have a chance of finding it unless you began with an idea of what kind of car you had. Are these wise men and wise women communicating to that place within yourself that knows Truth already, that place that is already free? The wise people are actually teaching you, or through them you are learning, about the spiritual being that you already are. They are helping you to remember your true nature which you have so often forgotten.

Those who have spoken to you have communicated ideas that sometimes appeared to contradict the words of one of the other teachers. Even if they did not contradict, you realize it would be impossible to actually take all of their suggestions to heart literally. Yes, in the midst of all of this great wisdom, you are seeing that ultimately you have to decide what you are going to do with your life. When it comes down to how to live your own life, even the greatest of wise people can only suggest and point. The highest wisdom from without would have no impact unless it resonated with that same wisdom within. You know you are alone, even when surrounded by the greatest of love. Great love and great solitude existing simultaneously. Inspiration is being given, you realize, but only you can choose to listen to it. And IT is now known to be your own Inner Voice. The teachers speak to you not only with their voices, but they speak to you with your own inner voice as well. How else could you have understood? Suddenly, the gap between you and these other beings disappears, and now you feel the unity rather than the aloneness. In no time you find yourself moving back and forth between Unity and Solitude.

You are being taught to receive guidance. Now, that voice within that you had sometimes listened to and often ignored, is seen for the powerful Guide that it really is. You would bow down to it in this instant, except you know it is not outside of you. Still, you bow to your teachers in appreciation, but no longer out of fear. You grasp the paradox. As above, so below. As without, so within.

The feared God above still lives in our heritage, and this idea is dying , but it takes much time as so much of the world still lives under the oppression of extreme poverty and lack of opportunity for education. Even in the so-called modern societies, man is having to constantly grow beyond ancient concepts which portray God as a separate other, usually male in form or attribute, who we must somehow relate to. This fits in well with our needs to maintain parent/child authority relationships which do not support our real growth but instead, these relationships keep us eternally separated from ourselves and one another.

Spiritual teachers and teachings are meant to awaken us to what is already true of us. It can be helpful to have inspirational people to listen to and read about, since they help us to aspire to our own spiritual growth. If the greatest ski jumping coach in the world came to you and told you the secrets of achieving a record breaking jump, it would do you little good unless you were already a dedicated and well trained ski jumper. Only an experienced jumper would truly understand the truth of what the coach was saying. The teacher can only appeal to your own state of readiness.

Something begins to happen when you start to experience this realization that no matter how many external guides you may have, or how many internal guides you may relate to, you alone are ultimately responsible for what you do or don't do, and what you listen to or don't listen to. It is not that you are independent, because you clearly are not. Yet, within the paradox of life you find yourself completely responsible for your own life at the very same time that you are totally dependent upon a mindboggling array of variables. This is the experience of the seamless nature of life. The rules and expectations of our modern life, our social hierarchies, our religious and moral codes, begin to appear so humorous that they cannot be taken seriously any longer. You are being in the world but not of it.

The idea is not to become independent, so that you no longer have any need for the teachers in the room, but your relationship to them and to life changes. You can now start to attend to the unique dimension of your life. Your calling. Your purpose. As you really begin to hear the special message that life has for you, you may experience great feelings of alienation from the life you have grown accustomed to. You may have one foot in your familiar life, while your other foot is trying to walk the path suggested by your higher nature. This draws you into the process known as the dark night of the soul. You higher calling, your higher nature, is in conflict with the dictates of your habitual or lower nature.

Yes, there is something very wonderful about the imagery of meeting the people of wisdom. Haven't we all longed at some moment for a divine intervention in our lives? Still, we must be ready to engage in holy war with our lower nature. It is not a matter of trying to be moral, or trying to live like a saint. It is much more personal than that. We may be more prepared than we realize to follow the appeals of our higher nature. The frustration that we feel when we ignore our higher calling is not a punishment imposed upon us by a distant and fearsome God. Our frustration stems from our own awareness that we want to start living differently. What it is that we are supposed to do will be absolutely unique for us. We may not find anyone who has been called to do exactly what we are called to do. We can draw inspiration from the lives of the saints, but we cannot mimic them and hope to hit the mark. We must hear our calling, enter the open road of our life, and take on our unique adventure, whatever it may be.

III

There are two major diversions presently facing people who are moved from within to embrace the inspired life, and they are both forms of mass conformity. One I call the religious diversion, and the other is what I will call the material diversion. The history of religion, like the history of man in general, is marked by movements of mass conformity. Even though the primary sources of inspiration, such as Jesus the Christ and Gautama the Buddha, seemed to have lived very unique lives, the religions which sprung up in their wake were largely mass movements.

Religion for the average man and woman is often comprised of attending church, or going to visit the ashram or temple. Thousands may enter and leave, and never leave a mark that speaks to their personal uniqueness. In fact, religion seems to have a difficult time with the individual, especially with the creative individual. Mass movements appeal to the mass man or woman. When someone begins to wake up, they find it more difficult to merely follow like a sheep. Strangely enough, the lives of those who have been held up as examples of spiritual courage are generally not lives that are conformist at all. Yet, freedom is often the first thing to be lost as soon as a religion is formed.

In the modern Christian era, Thomas Merton stands out as a writer and monk who did much to bring life back to a tradition that had lost its appeal for many churchgoers. Merton was influential, not because he conformed and followed the crowd, but precisely because he did not. His life was apparently a struggle with finding the balance between the collective life of a Trappist monk and the very individual life of the creative writer and poet. His struggle with these two directions is very much the same struggle facing many today. Part of growing up involves leaving the nest. At some point you must remove the training wheels from the bicycle if you are ever going to really ride. All of us are called by the urge to be free to step out into the unknown of our own lives.

It is as if we are all wearing veils, as though it were spiritually incorrect to let the light of our individuality shine. This conflict between the individual and the collective is ancient of course. As the Western world enters the 21st century, we see the pendulum swinging once again. We are critical now of too much individualism, and community is the buzz word of the day. Yet, there is something unconvincing about this trend. As trends move back and forth more quickly, it is easier to see them for the superficial movements that they actually are. Public opinion is so rapidly swayed now. First the masses think this, and now they think that. Eventually, if you want to be serious, you are forced to ignore these trends and dive deeper into the matter of living your life. Yes, only by stepping back from the mass movement can you really face your own life, and only then can you truly find your role in the collective. Criticisms of individualism are of little value, just as are criticisms of cooperative ventures. Obviously both are necessary. What must be criticized are the movements of neurotic individualism which are merely selfishness, and the movements of mass conformity in which individuals forsake their responsibility to apply their intelligence to the issues at hand and think for themselves. Following the crowd and appearing to cooperate is no virtue if the individual is not able to also stand alone if necessary.

It is much easier to see the selfish nature of those who emphasize their individuality, and so they have always been an easy target for those who are more comfortable living faceless lives of mass conformity. Yet, who more inspires us than the man or woman who overcomes great odds to live a life of commitment and intensity. If spirituality is about freedom, then the individual must stand and be creative. If spirituality is about love, then all efforts must move in the direction of service to others. Both must be present.

A difficulty confronts us as we face this matter of individual creativity. It is as if we live in a house of mirrors, and things are not what they appear to be. What looks like service to others, is often performed out of fear and conformity, and what looks like a selfish impulse can really be the gesture of freedom and true service. Many times people will feel immense guilt about actually living their own unique lives. Seldom have the ashrams or monasteries or churches openly accepted the creativity of their members. Creative figures of religious life have had to face great opposition from their various orders. Letting one's light shine is viewed with suspicion if not downright condemnation. Why? It is well known that religion has been used as a tool of both church and state. It is very difficult to control people when they learn to think for themselves. The teachings of Jesus and Buddha and other great spiritual masters turn us to truth, and they challenge us to live wisely and to outgrow our self-centered orientation. They do not invite us to simply join the crowd and follow blindly. We are not merely victims of the religious orders, however. We must assume responsibility for our own role in turning our backs on our own lives.

The religious life holds ideals up before us, like molds, and we then try to pour ourselves into one of these molds and hope that it fits. Christianity emphasizes service to humanity, and if you are going to be spiritual you find yourself comparing your life to storybook versions of the saints. You must go and feed the poor and so on. Secular life, on the other hand, holds up the material ideal. Either you have your own business or you are linked with power via a corporation, university, hospital, etc., etc.. The ideal of secular or material life revolves around comfort, status, security, and a sense of belonging. Your tribal status is marked by the clothes you wear, the car you drive and your dwelling. The religious ideal and the material ideal are so powerfully placed in our psyches, that we are probably mimicking them or reacting to them anytime we try to examine how we would like to live our lives.

These two influential models form part of the static we must begin to tune out as we attempt to listen to the messages from our soul. It is very true that life purpose is linked with our higher nature, and that our higher nature is characterized by love and not selfishness. Therefore, purpose and giving do go hand in hand, but that does not mean that your way of giving will look anything like what Mother Teresa is doing in Calcutta, for example. Certainly, Mother Teresa is following her heart's calling, but you must follow your heart's calling, and to do this you must listen to your higher self. You cannot hope to copy another's life. This is a very important part of a true process of discernment.

What if you want to work with people, and teach, counsel, etc.? You could join the peace corps, or you could become a major leader in the human potential movement and be paid a lot of money just to speak to people. You can fly all over the world and be in high demand. The ego will chew on these dichotomies, and you will find yourself flipping back and forth between channels. Perhaps you relate to this. Your options will actually be diametrically opposed to one another; although, there will be some kind of connecting thread that allows you to continually entertain these options. This can go on for years and a lifetime.

We want to be like Gandhi, but we also want to be famous like Gandhi, but we don't want to acknowledge that we want to be famous. It is very humbling to really begin to see what it is you want out of life. There is absolutely nothing wrong with these desires, but they must be sorted out. When we don't want to be godlike, and save the world, we want to be very successful in an overt material manner. We want power and money. No doubt. Do you have any of these movements inside of you? It is not uncommon for people who really desire power to not know that they want power. It is equally common for people who seem to wield power in our society to feel very insecure underneath all of their trappings of success. For this reason, the true expression of life purpose must always contain a match between the voice of the soul and the outer actions in the manifest world. We must sort through all of this baggage, and we will not be allowed to rest until we do.

Grandiosity and inferiority are two other poles that people move between. Perhaps the hidden and unclaimed desire is to be famous and powerful, while the surface personality of the individual is one that exudes humility and a lack of assertiveness. Some people are unhappy with their role in life because they have not claimed the power that they need to actually express their true purpose. Dissatisfaction haunts them until they begin to see that they really can do something if they only take steps to do it. True humility is not the product of keeping your light under a bushel. True humility can only appear when you have faced the truth about yourself. Humility is to be open to your soul's dictates rather than those of your ego. Humility is accepting the facts about yourself and not your ego's grandiose or demeaning opinions about yourself. If you need to be in charge and be a leader, then you must bow to this requirement and step into those shoes. To deny your true role has nothing to do with spirituality. Accept your true role. For many people that will mean stepping up to greater responsibility and greater creativity and greater power than they ever dreamed possible. This is not grandiosity. Grandiosity is to believe that your ego can tell your soul what to do. To surrender is not to put down your power, your intelligence, your talent. To surrender is to become an instrument of the Divine so that your talents can be used in the best way possible, regardless of what those talents are.

Perhaps it can be compared to graduating from painting by the numbers, where you follow the predetermined directions, and must paint between the lines and use the colors already selected for you. At some point you begin to obey a different set of instructions, and find yourself abandoning the paint by the numbers method, and you begin to paint freehand, following a set of more mysterious and less concrete instructions. You may be ready to graduate to a more creative and a more surrendered disposition than you realize. Many people today are sincerely trying to explore ways to serve mankind, and they are becoming volunteers within the many organizations out there that utilize volunteers to offer services of all kinds. This is a fine movement; however, when you look beyond the surface appearance of this movement and actually talk with many of these people, you begin to see a different picture.

While volunteering is a perfect outlet for one person, for another it is too much like painting by the numbers.

Often you must link up with an organization that operates very much like the conventional workplace. The volunteer job descriptions inform you what you can and cannot do, and you basically must paint between the lines. If you are at a place in your life where you are being prompted by strong internal cues to begin to manifest your unique form of life purpose, you may find, as many people in this position have, that it just is not going to work to follow someone else's set of guidelines as to what you can or cannot do. The impulse to serve draws you to the volunteer site, but once there you can discover that it just is not the right match. People in this situation can try over and over again to find a ready made outlet for their talents, only to discover again and again that they are going to have to assume a higher degree of power and creativity than they thought. They are going to have to create something themselves.

Now is the time when many new enterprises are in need of creation. Some of you will work within the system that already exists, but others will have to actually create the outlets for your talent. What you want to do just will not fit into the preexisting molds, and you will have to constantly compromise yourself if you do try to fit your vision within these molds. This dilemma is mentioned here only because it occurs quite frequently, and not as a criticism of the work that is done by established organizations. It is just that established organizations are just that, established.

Surrender is too often seen as giving up what you want because it is good for you to do so. This is not surrender. Surrender is an ongoing process of discrimination wherein you discover that what you used to want is no longer of interest to you, and that something else, something higher or more significant to your soul's development, is now of greater interest. While these two impulses battle with one another, your job is to surrender to the emerging greater interest. During one period of your life, surrender may be equated with following precisely the directions of a particular teacher. Later in your life, you find yourself moved to leave this teacher and follow a new voice. Is it surrender to stay with the teacher or to leave the teacher. It must be evaluated from within and not based upon external appearances. Perhaps it is time for you to obey a new and emerging voice. It is time to graduate. Graduation is not always accompanied by a grand ritual where you are patted on the back for your success. Sometimes graduation requires that you oppose the wishes of those who would pat you on the back, and take to the lonely road for a period of time. The rite of passage may involve your leaving the pack, and there is no way to experience this other than doing just that. If your teacher came to you and said it is now time for you to take leave, this would not give you the experience of surrendering to your internal guidance. This kind of choice is very often made in the face of opposition and great conflict. You must face the gods and say "No". Only later will you find out if the gods were secretly pleased with your courage to step out and leave the nest. Perhaps you will find out, but only later.

You are are not being asked to surrender to a foreign power that is distant and unfamiliar. That is a perception that can arise; yet, you are really surrendering to your own

Self, your own Higher Nature. Thus it will feel extremely intimate. You might find yourself simultaneously experiencing your own uniqueness and a sense of belonging to a whole. There is often a mood of detachment or indifference towards the results of your actions at the same time that you are being more creative and more effective than ever in your outer life. These two apparently contradictory experiences can occur because you are surrendered to your calling rather than trying to manipulate your calling to serve the needs of the ego.

A very important point to emphasize again is that we can fool ourselves to such an extent that we will move everywhere but the direction that we really want to be moving in. If you try to apply concepts of karma yoga, for example, to your life, you may very well begin to try to fit yourself into the religious mold. When we think of service, certain old connotations emerge that are nothing more than concepts. We think of humility, giving more than we receive, living a simple life, working for the disenfranchised, engaging in humanitarian acts, and so on. Though admirable, when applied from the outside as a mere belief system, something to conform to, you actually do violence to the unique voice inside of you. If you trusted that voice you would likely find that it will take you in the direction of the holy life without an effort to try and be holy, or spiritual, or kind.

Your true power, intelligence, and creativity will not be brought into full play if you ignore your inner voice and only accept a lesser direction provided by someone else or by some ancient religious teaching that was given in a different time and place. Spiritual types are quick to surrender their power; yet, this is not self-transcendence if their habit is to downplay their abilities anyway. For those who are already lacking confidence in their God-given talents, self-transcendence might look very different from the storybook religious version. What if you surrendered to your God-given abilities and accepted the challenge that they hold before you? What if you did not use religion to hide from your power and creativity? What if real humility, not neurotic self-hatred, resulted from allowing yourself to be moved by life as life wants to move you?

If you are at a place in your life where you feel great pressure to manifest your purpose, you should know that to not surrender to your calling is not an act of passivity. It takes great energy, great self-suppression, to hold back the creative force. You may want to ignore your calling, but that act of avoidance, if you could only see it clearly, is actually an act of great violence against yourself. The creative force is very powerful, and our habits of self-denial must be equally forceful to keep ourselves down. You must really choke the life out of yourself if you want to keep your calling hidden. This is just a matter of noticing, a matter of mindfulness, of seeing what you are really doing to yourself.

Spirituality is about having life more abundantly. It is really not about hiding your uniqueness under the covers of religious conformity. The Bible, the Bhagavad Gita, the Dhammapada, and the other great holy writings are not detailed accounts of how people are supposed to become mindless clones who all act the same way. These books expand us and open us beyond the little shell that we so often want to crawl under and claim as only our own. These books are not meant to tell you precisely what food to eat today, what work to do today, what goals to set today. These books point us towards our essential freedom, and from the point of view of freedom we will then make choices that fit the time and place of our lives. Freedom does not mean mindless individual expression. Freedom is actually the great siren call that our soul is longing to follow. Freedom equals great energy and creativity. Conformity, in the guise of community or cooperation, is really just a way station along the path.

As spiritually inclined people recoiled from the emphasis on materialism and career in the '60s and '70s, and really up to the present, they spent more time with meditation, study of spiritual texts, and so on. Many of those same people are now preoccupied with their "life purpose". More specifically they want to know what they are supposed to do. To be more than just another swing of the pendulum, something must change. What must change is our concept of spiritual life. Ultimately there is only life. There is no spiritual life and ordinary life. There is only life. At this confusing moment in time we are embracing contradictions without even knowing it. While many are interested in their life purpose, they also want to embrace the new romance of "ordinary life". Since the extraordinary life, that of spiritual exploration and esoteric practice, did not do it for us, perhaps we missed the boat, it is thought. Let's now embrace ordinary life. So, we now have this bizarre pot of values and motivations. There is unique purpose, ordinary life, a quest for community because we are all so lonely, a desire to escape the mindlessness of the ordinary job, and on and on. We try to entertain absolutely every option except the one that life is trying to hold before us. We do not want to act on that option.

There is absolutely nothing special about ordinary life. What is ordinary life? What is spiritual life? We create these ideas, and then suffer as we try to piece together the jigsaw puzzle of our broken lives. We experience the lack of sacredness in life, and then try to be sacred. We experience our lack of meaning, and then create a strategy to obtain meaning. Milarepa's statement, "My religion is to live and die without regret."[1], is turning us to our own life. "Ordinary life", now becomes a new category of experience. If answering phones all day long is boring you to death, do you really want to call that ordinary life, and try to romanticize it? Perhaps you are experiencing a mind numbing boredom because your soul wants to express what it needs to express in this life. There is nothing inherently right about answering phones, teaching school, managing an organization, etc. There is also nothing inherently wrong with these activities. You cannot merely call these activities ordinary life, and then claim to somehow understand what they are. Your life must be taken as a unique expression. For one person self-transcendence means staying where they are for the time being, but for another they need to break away and do things that will look selfish to themselves and those around them. Where is ordinary life and spiritual life in this kind of situation?

Is there a voice within you that has been sending you a consistent message for many years now? It keeps pointing out a life direction for you, but just as consistently you have resisted it. What if that voice is the voice of Life, the voice of God? What if the holy books are really trying to get you in touch with that voice within you? What if you are looking everywhere for suggestions on how to live, but have turned your back on the most intimate instruction of all? What if you began to listen to that voice, and actually risked acting upon its advice, even if things don't turn out the way you want them to? What if you reach a point where you know you have no choice but to listen to that voice? You know it is not going to be easy. It may be the greatest struggle of your life, but at least it is the struggle of your life. True enough, you are part of a whole, but it is also true enough that you cannot experience that wholeness unless you do play your part in the whole. Life is guiding us to this understanding. The reward is that we are returning home when we embrace the truth of our life. We are being turned to enjoy the seamless nature of existence wherein all is holy and the divisions drop away.

The idea that being and doing are separate modes
of operating has made it more difficult to be clear
regarding action in the world and the issue
of life purpose.

Action reveals your state of consciousness. Actions, (your thoughts, words, and deeds), are to be guided by your heart. "Lay not up for yourselves treasures upon earth, where moth and rust doth corrupt, and where thieves break through and steal: But lay up for yourselves treasures in heaven, where neither moth nor rust doth corrupt, and where thieves do not break through nor steal: For where your treasure is, there will your heart be also" (Matt 6: 19-21). As your consciousness, your heart, rises above the market place mentality, that of mere convention and materialism, you will find yourself compelled to change your actions. You will be driven to manifest a new and higher purpose. Purpose is nothing more than action which is aligned with the highest awareness that you are actually capable of being responsible for at any given period in your life. Your real capacity for responsibility may exceed your estimation.

When you prevent your action from being guided
by your highest light and wisdom, then
you experience meaninglessness and emptiness.
Then temptation arises to fill your time with
dead activities. You stay "busy". One action is
not inherently better than another. Action cannot
be evaluated separately from the individual
performing the action and the circumstance of the
action. Though one form of "work" cannot in
general be compared in value with another, if
you are blocking the expression of a form of work,
service, creation, that your soul longs to enact,
then you will experience a split in your nature.
If you resist your calling, that resistance will be
felt as separation.

Since being and doing are two sides of the One Coin of Life, they are dependent upon one another. Growth in one does not occur without growth in the other. Real growth in meditation will be matched with signs in one's external life of action. Semitic or "Western" faiths have tended to emphasize the outer moral and religious behavior, and the Eastern faiths have tended to emphasize the internal landscape and minimize action in the external world. This tendency to split being and doing, contemplation and action, is no longer a useful concept.

Your life purpose is not a separate item on life's menu. It is life! Milarepa, the Tibetan Yogi, knew this when he said, "My religion is to live and die without regret." His statement neither points us in an interior direction exclusively nor in an exterior direction. It points us to the seamless nature of existence AND, it invites us to LISTEN. To live and die without regret implies that we must live up to an Expectation. We must listen to our Inner Voice, our own Heart. We must ultimately answer to our Self, our True Nature.

How to end the split between your spiritual life and daily life? Though you can say that your spiritual life and daily life are one, you cannot really experience this wholeness, this seamless condition, unless you live and die without regret. This is our challenge, and it is uniquely personal. When you trust life, you listen to your hunches. You listen to that Voice or Intuition which you sense to be the voice of your higher nature. Only when you listen to your hunches, and follow them, can you truly say that you are experiencing the seamless nature of existence. Usually, we are split from ourselves. Our Inner Voice says to do such and such, but we hesitate and follow our habitual routine instead. We receive guidance, but we ignore it. Hence, we feel separate from life.

When your Inner Voice and your actions line up, then you experience something which is attractive. It is balance and harmony. It is proper function, and those moments stand out in contrast to the many other moments in which that balance is not present. Wholeness does not come and go, but your experience of it can.

Manifest existence continually phases. Success and failure eventually follow one another, as does life and death, ease and difficulty, and so on. It is not true that merely because you are following your sense of purpose in life that everything will then go smoothly in your external life or your internal life. That Peace which surpasseth understanding does just that. It surpasses understanding. Spiritual growth does not mean that you no longer have difficulties. It is a process in which that Peace, which is not dependent upon your mental state, emotional state or physical state, becomes an increasingly absorbing reality for you. The Kingdom of God, where Peace surpasses all understanding, is not of the world of changes. You live in this world but are not of it.

We especially lose contact with the seamless
nature of existence when we are active.
Many meditators have experienced peace
in their rooms only to find themselves unsettled
when they returned to the active life. We cannot
escape the life of action, no matter what we do.
We must face the conflict between being and
doing until we come to peace with
the apparent dichotomy. This is not easy.
Says Lord Krishna in the Bhagavad Gita, "Even
sages have been confused by the meaning
of 'active' and 'inactive'. Therefore I shall
explain what action is. Knowing this
will free you from evil."[2]

You can be inspired by the lives of the Saints and Sages, but life only asks you to live out your purpose. You cannot escape the role you are here to play, nor would you want to if you truly understood its importance to yourself and others. Your soul has been communicating with you for the entirety of your life, trying to guide your life so that heart and action are in alignment and move as one dynamic unit. Thus real devotion and surrender is marked by courage. The courage spoken of here is the courage to live the life you are called towards. You cannot evaluate your courage by comparing yourself with an other. You are not competing with anyone. Courage is a gift of Grace. It is when heart and action join hands.

Your desire for communion with the Godhead is not and cannot be separate from your desire to act in life. All great masters have acted in one form or another. They, like yourself, have a purpose to fulfill. Hildegard von Bingen, the Christian mystic, is said to have experienced spiritual conversion when she made the firm resolve to begin to write about her mystical experiences. Her decision took courage, since she lived in a powerful patriarchal world which discouraged women from speaking out.

* * * * * * * *

Eventually, you must admit to yourself that you do know what you are here to do. Of course, it seems odd to admit this if you are confused and full of doubt. It could be said another way: At any moment you are fully capable of knowing what to do. This is not to deny that dark periods exist in which you cannot see very far in front of you. All seems to be dying around you in these times, and you have no sense of where to turn next. When this time passes however, you will see that you were really not as lost as you presumed. These periods of darkness and unknowing allow you to reach that desperate place in which the only recourse is to surrender, which will be synonymous with knowing. It is darkest right before the dawn.

To experience knowing your purpose you must begin to practice acting upon the directives of your Inner Voice. You may hesitate, quite naturally, as you are not sure that your Inner Voice is correct. You will never know in advance if your Inner Voice is correct. If you knew in advance there would be no need for faith and trust. There would be no need for growth. Following your Inner Voice as best as you can will bring its own wisdom. Outcomes will not always be what you had hoped for, and you may even doubt that you did the right thing. Nonetheless, there is no option other than to continue listening to that Voice and acting upon it. Even if you feel betrayed by it, you will find absolutely nothing and no one else to turn to.

We do not see that our moments of clarity
regarding the action to be carried out next
are but steps along the way. These moments of
clarity will be replaced by moments in
which the future appears dim, and
these moments replaced by future moments
of clarity once again. The still point, the
Kingdom of God, contains all of these
cycles without complaint or celebration.
This is the Ideal which we can be moved by.
Our practice is to notice when we are caught
up in the drama of the changes, either good or bad,
and return as best we can to that still point
of peace. Of course we will fail in this again
and again, but we are also capable of
remembering again and again. And each
time we remember our faith becomes a
bit stronger. We learn for ourselves that
the Light really is shining all of the time,
and that the experience of darkness is a
sign of forgetfulness and not a sign of
how things really are.

Your higher nature is not impressed with
doubts and fears or social imperatives. It is free.
Therefore, when your creativity and your
higher nature join forces, you will act.
It can happen anytime; yet, it seems to only
happen when the time is right. Both are true.
You cannot rush the sprouting of the seed,
but you can certainly plant it and tend it,
and be present to experience its growth.
When you are ready, you can begin to manifest
your purpose. You can start writing the book now.
You can make that phone call now. You can
detail your proposal now. When you are ready
and the time is right, then you can act and you
will be free in your action. What can stop you
after all, when you are not concerned with
failure nor desperate for success. You are free to act.
Each action will carry its own reward.
You will be guided by your own experience.
You have stepped into the sacred river of your life.

Marketplace consciousness is the consciousness
of the lower nature. The lower nature is
only an illusion created by our insistence
upon asserting our separateness. Nonetheless,
it can be a convincing illusion.
BUT IT IS NOT THE TRUTH!
Your purpose cannot manifest through
the marketplace consciousness. Marketplace
consciousness does not want to surrender
to the Inner Voice or Christ Consciousness.
It wants to be sly and negotiate with it,
if it acknowledges it at all.
You cannot negotiate with your calling.

Your talents can be directed by either the lower or higher nature. When directed by the lower nature, your talents may lead you to success, but you will feel the inflation of self-importance which is nothing more than separation. When directed by your higher nature, you may feel as if you are a being moved by an intimate other. You suddenly are moved and inspired to surrender, but surrender to what. The language varies with the report of the experience. Some say they surrender to God, others say they are following an inner guide, and then others are simply following their heart. In all cases the inner and outer have joined. Heart and action become one. In this seamless experience true humility can emerge. Only when you are truly being yourself does identification with the "I" drop away. Only when you surrender to your higher nature do you experience purpose and meaning. Meaning and inspired function go together.

Are you looking for results which will justify the following of your life purpose? What results did Jesus look for? It could be said that Jesus followed his heart, and look at the horrible events which befell him. He was crucified for his efforts. This type of evaluation is a product of the lower nature. The lower nature will masquerade as common sense or practical thinking and say things like, "Jesus threw caution to the wind in order to follow his heart, and look what it brought to him. I'd better not follow his example." The lower nature wants to negotiate and pursue safety; it is ignorant of the fact that the safety it pursues does not exist. Real spiritual security comes from the recognition of our true nature; yet, our lower nature does not take solace in the truth. The lower nature finds its sense of security in those things that only come and go, like money, status, and possessions. The lower nature cannot manifest true life purpose.

It is said in Ecclesiastes that, "There is an appointed time for everything, and a time for every affair under the heavens. .... A time to seek, and a time to lose; a time to keep, and a time to cast away" (3:1,6). You may act according to your highest truth and still find yourself ill, unemployed, going through divorce, etc. Following your life purpose does not mean that from now on only positive appearing events will occur in your life. In fact, it is striking how often people begin to follow their heart while in the midst of some of the most trying times of their lives. As you act according to your highest light you will find that action is its own reward.

The lower nature does not understand
this type of reward at all. The lower nature
lives in a fantasy and fears the cycles of
material existence. This is natural and not
something to feel guilty about. Over and over
again we will face fears in living out our lives.
It is just that our higher nature can show
us a different vision of the world and our
relationship to it. When living from this higher
vision we are in the world but not of it. As you
follow your higher nature as best you can,
you will taste moments of fearlessness,
moments of being guided, and moments
of being an instrument of a higher power.

To "know" your purpose is to live in a state of readiness. To know does not mean that you are always aware of exactly what you will be doing tomorrow. You may notice in hindsight that there is a distinct manner in which you are moved to express yourself in life. You may see that you play primary roles which are a cornerstone of your purpose. You might be a communicator, organizer, scientist, homemaker, or teacher of children. From hindsight you can see the themes of your life. It is not true that you are lacking direction like a leaf in the wind. Purpose is manifesting itself in you. You just have to notice it and then consciously cooperate with it.

You cannot escape the limits of the time and space in which you live. Part of any creative process is to work within the limits which are facing you. To deny limits is to live in fantasy. Anyone who has begun to follow their path of purpose has had to confront limits. However, as you begin to take action you will find the limits that the lower nature presumed to be real are not the real limits, and the actual limits begin to make sense to you, even though it may still require great energy and faith to deal with these limits. The actual hurdles that you must deal with will only be seen as you take action.

One of these limits is TIME. If your time is filled with functions that have nothing to do with your actual calling, then you can never begin. You may find that not only must you say, "yes", to your calling, but you must also say, "no", to other activities in your life. Until this is done, a calling can just remain an exciting idea that never takes shape. For this reason, to follow your calling with conscious intent marks a very distinct turning point in your life. Everything can change, and you may find yourself going through many periods of wanting to return to filling your time with the old stagnant routines of relationship, work, play, etc., etc,. You will only know as you take action what is actually required of you. You will be tested. How badly do you want to listen to your Inner Voice? Do you really trust it? What if you do not immediately see the results you had hoped for? Will you still be able to say, "Yes", when you must patiently face limitations? We are given endless opportunities, so it seems, to once again say, "Yes". Although, it has been said, that certain windows of opportunity must be grasped when they are available. To not grasp them is to lose them.

As often as you can, return to That of which
you are certain. Become still. What is more certain
than the fact of existence itself. Close your eyes.
Breathe fully and relax into the Silence. Notice
how rich and full the Silence is. Feel Silence
penetrating the core of your being.
"Be Still, and know that I am God."

The act which you carry out, the expression
of your purpose, is not important in itself alone.
If it were, you could earn your way to heaven,
so to speak. The living out of your purpose allows
you to function harmoniously as part of the
whole. Through surrendering to your role in life,
you will be making a contribution, and you
will experience a genuine sense of belonging.

Life purpose is relational. Energy is exchanged. It is not a private affair. You surrender to your calling and are called out into life in some manner that fits you and your life and circumstance. Life purpose is always relational. That is why your calling can be seen in terms of vocation rather than avocation. Vocation implies a powerful intention to apply your talent and energy in a specific manner, rather than a casual application of your abilities. You may or may not be financially rewarded for your actions. You must share or attempt to share your efforts in a manner such that others are served by that which you do.

Inspiration moves you and guides your talents. In the manifest world that which is created always takes a final shape. No matter how many prototypes you may make, eventually you have a finished copy. You may change it often, but at some point a product or service is packaged for sale or given as a gift. This is why sharing your talent is critical. When a song is sung before an audience, it is a finished product. You may improve on it later, but for that moment it is complete. You cannot experience the completeness unless your gift is given. It must be given as is, with its flaws and its attributes. Thus, your life purpose provides an excellent means for you to stay real, grounded, and humble. If you never give your gift away, you can live in fantasy. If you give your gift again and again and again, you will develop depth. It will be much easier to open yourself to intuitive guidance when you are in motion.

T he person who is suffering from a severe eating disorder may lose so much weight that they are actually in immediate danger of dying; yet, their internal perception is that they are overweight. Were you to meet a person in this situation, you would immediately perceive that they were seriously underweight. The concerns of the person with the eating disorder may revolve around efforts to lose even more weight. If this person were to express these concerns to you, it would probably be quite clear that the concerns could not be addressed in a direct and logical manner, because they stemmed from an internal misperception which was not yet recognized by the person involved.

This internal misperception is something similar to what we experience when we are not in touch with who we are and what we are here to do. This is not merely a psychological phenomenon. The misperception is visceral, felt, emotional, physical, and psychological. The soul is not experienced as only an otherworldly event; it is earthly as well as heavenly. It is rock, soil, water, lightning, thunder, cloud, sky, sun, moon and stars, mountain top and ocean beach. It simply is, and people the world round know this direct experience, for it is our most basic sense of life, harmony and balance. Only our preoccupation with the thinking mind makes us doubt this true gnosis. This direct knowledge not only informs us regarding who we are, in the most immediate sense, but it also guides us as to what we should be doing. When we lose touch with our direct identity, when we become split inside, we no longer hear the guidance of the soul, but instead we follow the fragmented voices, inside and outside, that lead us into directions and choices that may temporarily please our lower nature, but deep inside we can sense that we are not in touch with our true course. To feel guilty about this situation is really to miss the point, for this is clearly a developmental or evolutionary process. We cannot reach our next level of development without first passing through earlier levels. The suffering we have to put up with can be seen as growing pains. If we can be consciously and responsibly involved with this growth process, then we will become more mature as a result of the challenges we must face.

When we are out of touch with basic truths about ourselves, then we cannot even ask appropriate questions. We all experience this, at many various levels, within our individual lives. These basic truths are not cosmic only. As above, so below. The profound is expressed in the simple. God comes to us in the form of apple, breath and rain as well as in the forms of grand insights and angelic experiences. We forget who we are, and this is discovered in the simplest areas of our lives. We lose touch with how much we need to eat to sustain life, we lose touch with the fact that we love to paint, we lose touch with the reality that we really are creative and we perceive ourselves to be without real talent and inspiration. We see everyone else's talent, but we cannot perceive our own and accept our own and express our own.

We all need to be seen for who we really are, in the most basic truths about ourselves, by somebody who can truly perceive that dimension which is hidden from us. We need others in order to truly perceive ourselves. Special people are sent into our lives to help us to know who we are, and we are sent to others to help them to know who they are, and in this way the light is passed from individual to individual. The nature of this illumination is precise and uniquely appropriate for the individual being touched.

When you are not in touch, literally, in the most visceral sense of that word, with your soul's direction, then you are off course. Your questions will reflect your confusion and not your clarity. Hence, even if you were to answer your questions intellectually, it would really do no good. You may ask, "What is it that I am supposed to be doing with my life?", and even if you were told the answer it would not really change things. We literally lose touch with that which is <u>most</u> obvious about ourselves, and this is what we need to once again identify with, and it occurs in the same way a tennis player finally feels what it is like to hit an effortless, yet powerful backhand stroke. It is felt. You finally wake up and connect with what you want to do. You feel it in your bones. It is true about you, perhaps always has been, and you are just waking up and saying, "Yes", to what is really obvious. You simply accept your talent and the worthiness of that talent, and the fact that there is something that you love to do. All of your doubts, which may still exist, start to lose their power in the face of the direct acceptance of who you are. This acceptance occurs simultaneously with your acting upon your inner guidance. Step two is revealed only after you take step one, and step three is indicated only after step two.

At first, it may come to you in moments and then fade away, but once you start to feel it, you will be brought back again and again. Once you reconnect with what is most obvious and true about you, then your questions will start to have power and meaning. You will no longer be a coyote who is wondering how to fly, but instead, you will be a coyote who enjoys a natural fleetness of foot and you can begin to participate in the gift that has been given to you. You will know the rightness of this; it will feel right. It may also feel frightening because you are used to listening to the voice of the lower nature or the false self. The false self is nothing more than the confused self. It is not evil in the moralistic sense, but it is confused. The devil within is your own confusion, and when you are confused you do things that you really do not want to do.

When you fight your own nature, then God can only be a distant other. When you begin to allow the expression of your own nature, then suddenly God is so close that you cannot find the words to express the nearness. The spiritual path is therefore one of wholeness. Not a wholeness designed with conscious intent by man, but an already existing wholeness, gracefully given, to be enjoyed by us in a conscious manner. This wholeness, this gnosis, becomes the one Law which precedes all other laws. When the many laws are placed ahead of the one Law, it is a sign of our already confused state. When we awaken to the one Law, the one Wholeness, then all the other laws find their proper place. As you live a life that more fully expresses the soulful intent you were born with, you will be doing a great service to the world. A service that will extend far beyond the mere physical deeds that you perform. You will be demonstrating the Law in your life, and others will be touched by the spirit in which you live. This is what it means to give your life for your fellow man and woman. That you and all should have life and have it more abundantly.

The tendency to prefer being a spectator in life, rather than a participant, has probably been with mankind for ages. However, there may have never been more opportunities to exercise the spectator consciousness than now. We are invited into the fragmented lives of others via the electronic media, and countless books and magazines. At best, we can be inspired by the lives of others, but this type of inspiration is very often a temporary high which allows us to feel life a little more fully for a moment.

To have a purpose in your life and to have a few inspirational figures that you turn to because they provide inspiration that helps to move you along your own path is one thing. To have no sense of direction, and to endlessly stimulate yourself via the lives of others is another thing. One is not right and the other wrong; they are simply very different events. The fact that we do not often have frequent and direct experience in associating with people who are truly mature and conscious creates a problem that is very significant. We end up not knowing what the real process actually looks and feels like. We are forced to compare ourselves to the lives of people we have only read about or seen represented in movies and so on. Reading about someone or seeing a movie might be compared to watching a plant sprout, grow to maturity, and flower via time lapse photography. You can observe in minutes a process that may have actually taken many days to unfold. When you are unable to have contact with the real process, you do not develop an understanding of the actual pace and sensation of the process. Instead, you begin to compare your own development process to the images from books and movies, and you find that you always fall short. Many people, right now, are in the midst of some very important spiritual development, but they do not realize it. They are either tempted to evaluate their lives by criteria that the conventional world uses to judge success and achievement, or they can be tempted to compare themselves to the lives of historical spiritual men and women whom they have only read about.

From the point of view of the typical marketplace consciousness, the true maturation of a spiritual consciousness is something to be avoided like the plague. This is because it spells the death of the lower nature which is the root of materialism in the first place. You can still gain much from reading about the lives of those who have been through the process you are going through, but it is critical to keep in mind that you are being fed only bits and pieces about those persons' actual life, personality, and behavior. Hero worship can actually hold you back, at a certain point in your development.

Examples of how others have "done it" are very tempting, but remember that you may not be getting the whole story at all. I have read the many stories of people's transformation experiences, and I have also interacted with thousands of people. I am always amazed that I do not find these storybook versions of transformation represented in the lives of real flesh and blood people. When you meet the real person and hear the real story and the real struggle and how long things really took, you get an entirely different picture. These are the flesh and blood stories, and they are based in real time, not book time or movie time. The real stories are also not packaged in such a way so as to sell a book or video or cassette tape. As you understand this fact, then you are better able to use your discrimination when reading about the lives of others. You will also realize that regardless of what happened to someone else, you have your own life, and grace must manifest through it as it is.

In your imagination and your meditations you can contact peace and wisdom. Clearly, one of the great works facing mankind, is the constant work of bringing that peace into the the manifest world of our lives on Earth. Is not your individual role and unique purpose simply one of the critical facets of this great work? You cannot hope to single-handedly accomplish the great work, obviously. However, you can begin to resonate with this great work and see how your own unique role is a critical piece, small though it may be. Understanding this, and sensing this deep within yourself, will do at least two things for you. First, it will allow you to work energetically without collapsing from the despair that can arise when you view the immensity of the task facing mankind. You realize that the best thing that you can do is to do your part. You also see that you are not alone, and that is the second benefit of this understanding. You are not alone. You may feel that you are being torn from your old life, your old associations, your old life style, and this can be a very lonely experience. However, you will come to see that you are also being led to others, joining with others, joining with a grand network and evolving matrix of help that is both earthly and heavenly. This understanding will give you the courage to face those times when you feel you are making the biggest mistake of your life in following the guidance of your heart. It may very well be true that you are more committed than you realize to a great purpose. When the deeper dimension of your true self begins to surface and call the shots more and more, you will desire to walk the path of the open road more than anything else. Your purpose is about much more than you. It is about a great unfolding which involves your participation.

VII

Just because the life story and teachings of Jesus have been largely dominated by the Christian churches, does not mean that his teachings were meant to be used in the patriarchal and authoritarian manner which has been so common. The churches have typically claimed the right to be an intermediary between man and the wisdom that Jesus shared, but there is no reason for us to give any credence to this claim. Having said this, I would like to extend an invitation to contemplate the meaning and significance of the Lord's Prayer. This prayer is placed here as a superb example of a spiritual communication which affirms the Transcendental, and also directs men and women to give form to the Transcendental via the thoughts, words and deeds of their daily life. Since this prayer is a part of the heritage of so many people, it seems a very useful exercise to interact with this prayer and allow your own insight and understanding to merge with the words. Through your own meditation upon this prayer, you may find that it contains a message that applies directly to your life in this time and in this place.

"Our Father"

That One which has nurtured our soul,

whispered to us the secrets of the Heart,

and which has enlivened our body, mind,

and feeling nature. That One, at once impersonal

and seemingly distant and simultaneously

our closest Companion, Father, Mother, Lover,

Guide, and Tender Consoler who knows us

more than we ourselves do.

That One which surrounds us, lives us,

breathes us and ultimately is who we are.

We beseech that One.

"Who Art In Heaven"

That Place, that state of consciousness, in

which perfect love and harmony is

the ultimate law.

Heaven is not elsewhere, but is the condition

wherein the sacred order is acknowledged

and embraced.

Suffering and death do not contradict

the reality of Heaven, for suffering and death

are threats to our lower nature, which has

forgotten its true identity and seeks out a

false god in the world of objects and ownership.

When the Christ consciousness awakens,

suffering and death reveal themselves to

be of "this world" only. That One

which lives us is not separate from

the ultimate condition of harmony, or Heaven.

Hence, the Father is said to dwell in Heaven.

"Hallowed Be Thy Name"

Thy Name echoes from the depths of our soul and is voiced most clearly in profound Silence.

"Thy Kingdom Come.
Thy Will Be Done On Earth,
As It Is In Heaven."

*May Thy order become manifest in all
our lives. May we pierce the veil of
untruth and become instruments of Thy will.
May our soul be free to follow its purpose in
this time and place so that our unique
work and contribution may be done here.
May our work be blessed for it is the
outer reflection of Thy will, and is the
means for the transformation of
life on Earth.*

"Give Us This Day Our Daily Bread."

We affirm the truth which is so readily apparent to us.
We are daily given all that we have, and our
request acknowledges our reliance upon you,
the ultimate Giver, to whom we are indebted
for life itself. We gratefully ask of you,
and you generously give of your riches.

"And Forgive Us Our Trespasses, As We Forgive Those Who Trespass Against Us."

You have revealed to us the secret of

attaining peace on Earth.

As we follow your example, we learn one of

life's greatest lessons:

We are forgiven, released from bondage,

as we forgive others and ourselves.

"And Lead Us Not Into Temptation But Deliver Us From Evil."

Guide us to see beneath the surface of this world.
Help us to see with eyes of understanding
so that we do not mistake the merely temporary
for the real.
Let our thoughts, words and actions
be guided by our highest truth,
and lead us away from error
caused by our own misperceptions.

"Amen"

So Be It.

Notes

1   The Saying of Milarepa: "My religion is to live and die without regret." Quoted by Sogyal Rinpoche in *The Tibetan Book of Living and Dying* (Harper San Francisco, 1992)

2   The passage from the Bhagavad Gita: "Even sages have been confused by the meaning of 'active' and 'inactive'. Therefore I shall explain what action is. Knowing this will free you from evil." Translated by Kees W. Bolle, excerpted from *Universal Wisdom: A Journey Through The Sacred Wisdom Of The World*, by Bede Griffiths. (Fount, An Imprint of HarperCollins, 1994)

Please contact Morning Light Publications
if you have an interest in the following:

Arranging a group dialogue series
with the author in your area.

Placing your name on an events mailing list to receive
information regarding speaking events and/or audio-
taped conversations with Bernard Theroux.

Write to:

Morning Light Publications
P.O. Box 15341
Seattle, Washington 98115-0341

Or Call:

(206) 251-1050

About the Author

Prior to 1993 Bernard Theroux had lived a life that was largely divided between two passionate and apparently diverse pursuits. On the one hand he had helped several thousand people gain much needed insight into the nature of their unique talents and nurtured their pursuit of their personal creative potential. On the other hand he, like many others, had long been involved in the study of Eastern spiritual teachings. He became involved with several teachers who were important catalysts along the path.

In January, 1993, the nature of Bernard's work began to rapidly change following a spontaneous integration process which, having started in 1992, began to make a critical impact upon him. As the veil between the so-called worldly life and spiritual life lifted, he began to observe that the very concepts and expectations that people based their spirituality upon, whether of the East or West or combinations of the two, had themselves become the most significant barrier to spiritual evolution. Instead of taking refuge in the living truth which dissolves all that is built upon falsehood, many spiritual seekers have found themselves lulled into passivity by the very words which were meant to awaken them.

Bernard's teaching work and dialogues held with groups of interested people is an attempt to counter this trend.